Origins

Round-up

Gary Wilson ✶ **Jonatronix**

OXFORD
UNIVERSITY PRESS

In this story ...

Also ...

The Parker twins

Swan and cygnets

Chapter 1 – The Parker twins

Max, Cat and Tiger were heading towards their old micro-den, a hollowed out tree stump in the park. Tiger had challenged Max to a race in the micro-vehicles. Max was going to be in the micro-copter, Tiger in the micro-buggy. The first one to do a lap of the pond would be the winner. Cat was going to referee.

"I'm definitely going to win!" bragged Tiger.

"Not with the way you drive!" said Max.

"You're more likely to end up in the pond," giggled Cat.

Tiger scowled at them both.

Max heard footsteps on the path behind them. He turned round to see Ant running towards them.

"Guys," said Ant, breathless. "You have *got* to come and see this!"

"Not now, Ant," said Tiger. "We've got a race on."

Max was not quite as impatient as Tiger. "What is it, Ant?"

"It's the swan. The eggs have hatched!"

"Cool," said Cat. "How many babies are there?"

"Five," Ant said excitedly. He had been watching the swan carefully, ever since it had started to make a nest at the side of the large pond.

"Swans," moaned Tiger. "Is that all? I want to race!"

"Come on, Tiger," said Max. "It won't take long. Besides, you can check out the race course."

Tiger thought about it for a minute. "Well, OK … if we're quick."

Before long they reached the pond. Ant led them over to the far side, to where the tall rushes grew. They followed the path as it curved round the side of the pond. As they neared the rushes, they heard a dog barking. Then they heard the sound of laughter – harsh, grating laughter.

Max signalled for them to stop. They peeked round the rushes. Ant gasped. He could see two boys throwing stones into the pond – at the swan's nest. They had a dog with them. It jerked at its lead as it barked.

"Move it, swan," said one of the boys.

"Yeah, let's see your babies," said the other. "They'll make good target practice."

The swan hissed angrily. It stretched its wings out, trying to protect the baby cygnets.

Ant clenched his jaw. He took a step forwards but Tiger grabbed him by the shoulder.

"Hang on, Ant," said Tiger quickly. "You don't want to mess with them."

"Why," said Cat, who was almost as angry as Ant. "Who are they?"

"The Parker twins," explained Tiger. "Jack and Ben. They are in my brother's year at school. Toby says they're really tough bullies."

"I don't care who they are," said Ant. He could feel his anger bubbling like a shaken bottle of lemonade. "I won't let them hurt the swans." With that, he strode up to them. "Hey!" he called out. "Stop that!"

One of the boys, Jack, spun round. When he saw Ant, he grinned. "What do *you* want?"

"You're frightening them." Ant was too annoyed to be scared.

"Poor birdy," said Jack nastily. "And *what* are you going to do about it?"

"I … I," stammered Ant. He hadn't thought that far.

"Maybe we should use you as target practice instead?" said Ben. He tossed a stone up and down in his hand.

"Or maybe we should let Caesar off?" said Jack.

The dog growled at Ant, showing a row of sharp teeth.

"You leave him alone!" Cat shouted, striding towards them.

"Who's your *girlfriend*?" sneered Ben.

"Don't be idiots," said Cat.

Max and Tiger were behind her.

"Got your whole class here, have you?" scoffed Ben.
"Yes, actually," Max fibbed. "They're all just coming."
"Yeah, we're on a field trip," joined in Tiger, "to
study the swans."

Jack glared at them. "Come on, Ben," he said eventually. "We've got better things to do anyway." He barged past Ant.

Ant fell backwards on to the grass. The twins walked away laughing.

"Are you OK, Ant?" said Max, when they had gone. He pulled Ant to his feet.

"Fine," Ant grumbled. He brushed himself down and walked over to the edge of the pond.

With the two boys gone, the swan had settled back on its nest.

"I don't think they'll be back," Max said to Ant. "Not when they think lots of people will be here."

"Field trip! That was a good one, Tiger," laughed Cat.

"Well, they don't know our school's on half term, do they!" smiled Tiger. "Now then, what about this race?"

The four friends walked to their micro-den. Ant didn't want to go at first in case the bullies came back, but he realized he could not stay there all day.

Tiger saw that his friend needed cheering up.

"Come on, Ant," he said. "You can be in the race, too. You can ride in the micro-buggy with me. I need a co-pilot … to make sure I don't steer into the pond," he added, with a grin.

Cat told Ant that she would wait by the bin, near the tall rushes. "That way I can watch out in case the Parker twins come back," she explained.

Ant had smiled then. "OK," he agreed.

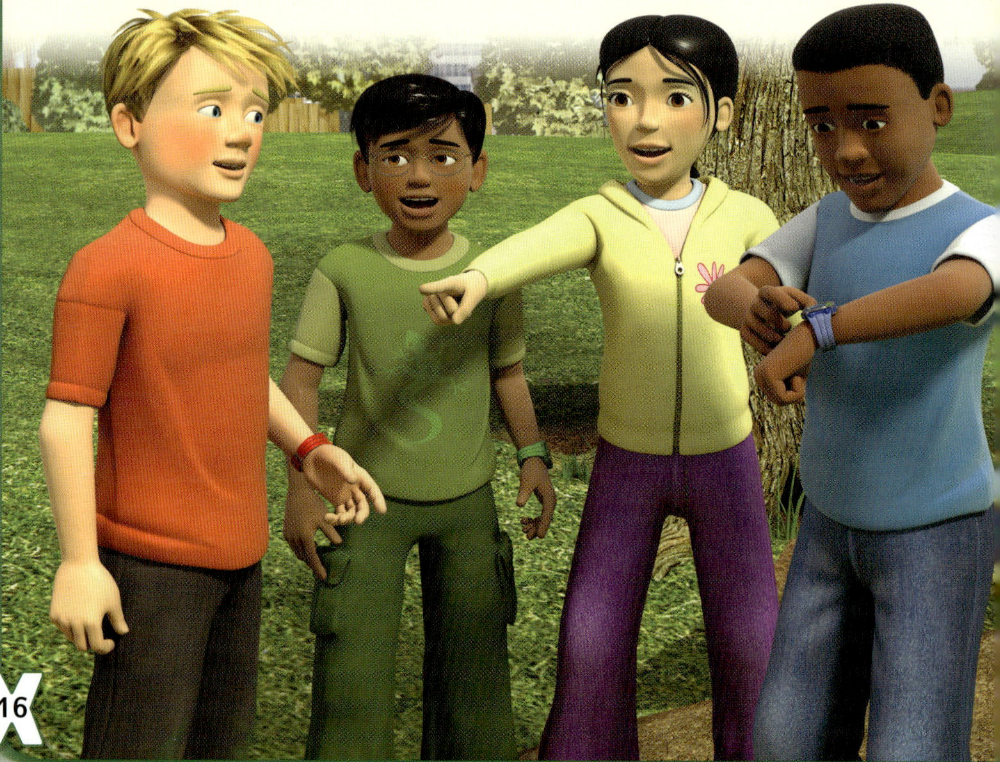

Max, Cat, Ant and Tiger turned the dials on their watches. They pushed the X and …

"Right," said Cat, "the first one to reach me will be the winner." She gave her home-made flag a wave. "And remember … I'll be watching, so no cheating!" she warned. She flipped up the top of her watch and showed them the tracking function with four coloured dots on.

"As if!" Tiger said innocently.

Cat jogged back to the pond while the boys checked their vehicles.

Max made sure the feather blades on the micro-copter were securely in place.

Ant checked the tyre pressure on the micro-buggy while Tiger checked the steering.

When they were ready to go, Max pulled on his helmet and strapped himself in. Ant and Tiger climbed into the micro-buggy and secured their seatbelts.

"Ready," called out Max, above the whirr of the blades.

"Set," shouted Tiger, revving the engine.

"Go!" yelled Ant.

They were off!

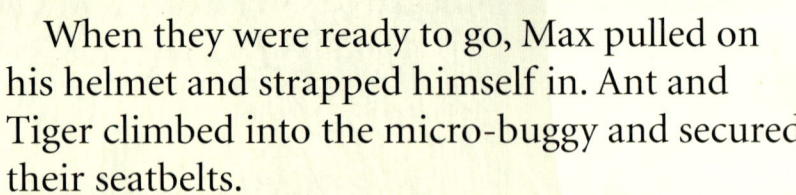

Go!

Chapter 3 – Caught

Cat was puffing by the time she reached the bin by the pond. She had run most of the way there. She picked a long, thin piece of grass and laid it across the path to mark the finish line.

Then she sat down to rest. The dots on her watch began to move, so she knew the race had started.

"They'll be ages yet," she thought. She yawned, stretched and closed her eyes.

Cat woke with a jolt. She heard a terrifying screech. It was accompanied by frantic splashing.

"The swan!" she gasped. Quickly Cat jumped up and looked around. She thought the Parker twins must have come back, but there was no sign of them or their dog.

She ran in the direction of the noise, round the bin and down to the edge of the pond.

There, she saw the swan thrashing frantically around in the water. At first she couldn't see what was causing it to panic. But then the swan jerked its head, and Cat could see that there was a loop of plastic round its neck. The other end was caught on to a branch.

"She'll strangle herself at this rate!" she said to herself.

Cat looked at her watch. The moving blue, green and red dots told her that the boys were still some way away. It was up to her to save the swan and … "The cygnets!"

She looked over to the nest. It was empty.

Chapter 4 – Cygnets on the loose

Tiger spun the steering wheel to the right.

"Watch out!" cried Ant, as they narrowly missed another rock.

"Stop shouting!" said Tiger. "You're making me nervous."

"I'm making *you* nervous!"

Tiger could see Max just ahead of him, in the micro-copter. He stamped down on the accelerator, and the micro-buggy shot forward.

Max was concentrating hard. They were round the halfway mark. He glanced over his shoulder and smiled. He had a good lead on Tiger. He saw Ant pointing at something ahead. He looked round … but it was too late.

SMACK! The smile was wiped from Max's face as he hit a large, soft, grey wall that had just appeared.

The micro-copter was sent spinning towards the ground. Max yanked back on the controls and the micro-copter slowed. He landed on the ground with a thump.

Tiger slammed on the brakes and the micro-buggy spun round in a circle. It bumped on to the grass and juddered to a halt, missing Max by millimetres.

Tiger and Ant jumped out of the micro-buggy. Both were shaking. They ran over to Max who was still lying on the ground.

"Ow," groaned Max.

"You OK?" asked Tiger.

"I-I think so. What happened?"

Tiger and Ant helped him up.

"It's the cygnets," explained Ant. "Look!"

He pointed at the five cygnets that had waddled out into the path.

"Where's their mum?" asked Max.

"I don't know," said Ant, worried. "She wouldn't normally leave them."

"They look a bit lost," said Tiger.

The cygnets began cheeping. They started to wander into the grass, away from the pond.

"Oh, no!" said Ant, alarmed. "They will definitely get lost if they go that way."

"We need to round them up," said Tiger.

The cygnets were waddling away quickly now.

"Let's go," said Max. He started the micro-copter … but didn't take off.

"Max, I don't think you're going anywhere," said Ant.

Max looked up. One of his feather blades had snapped in two.

Chapter 5 – Rescue attempt

Cat looked down and gulped. The water seemed a long way down. She was crawling along the branch that was overhanging the pond. The branch got narrower towards the end where the plastic loop was hooked on to it. Each time the swan flapped its wings, the branch shook. Cat held on tight.

Some people say that a swan's peck is so powerful it can break a person's leg. Cat knew this was nonsense. But now she was micro-size, she was not sure what damage the swan could do. And the closer she got to the thrashing swan, the less sure she became.

The swan looked up and saw Cat. It lunged towards her, snapping its beak. Cat threw herself flat on the branch, hugging it. The swan's beak just missed her.

"Whoa," Cat said to the swan, trying to calm it down.

Slowly, she started inching forwards again. She used her flag to push the plastic loop towards the end of the branch where it was hooked on. If she could push it off, the swan would be free.

"Nearly ... there," she said, stretching forwards as far as she could. "Nearly ... "

Cat gave a final push and the plastic flicked free of the branch. "That's it!"

Just at that moment, the swan jerked its head. The branch shook and Cat lost her balance. Suddenly there was nothing beneath her. She was falling.

Cat tumbled downwards.
"I've had it!" she thought.
But instead of landing with a splash as she had thought, she fell on to a soft, white bed of feathers. She had landed on the swan's back.
The swan gave a cry and flapped its massive wings … free at last.

Chapter 6 – Round-up

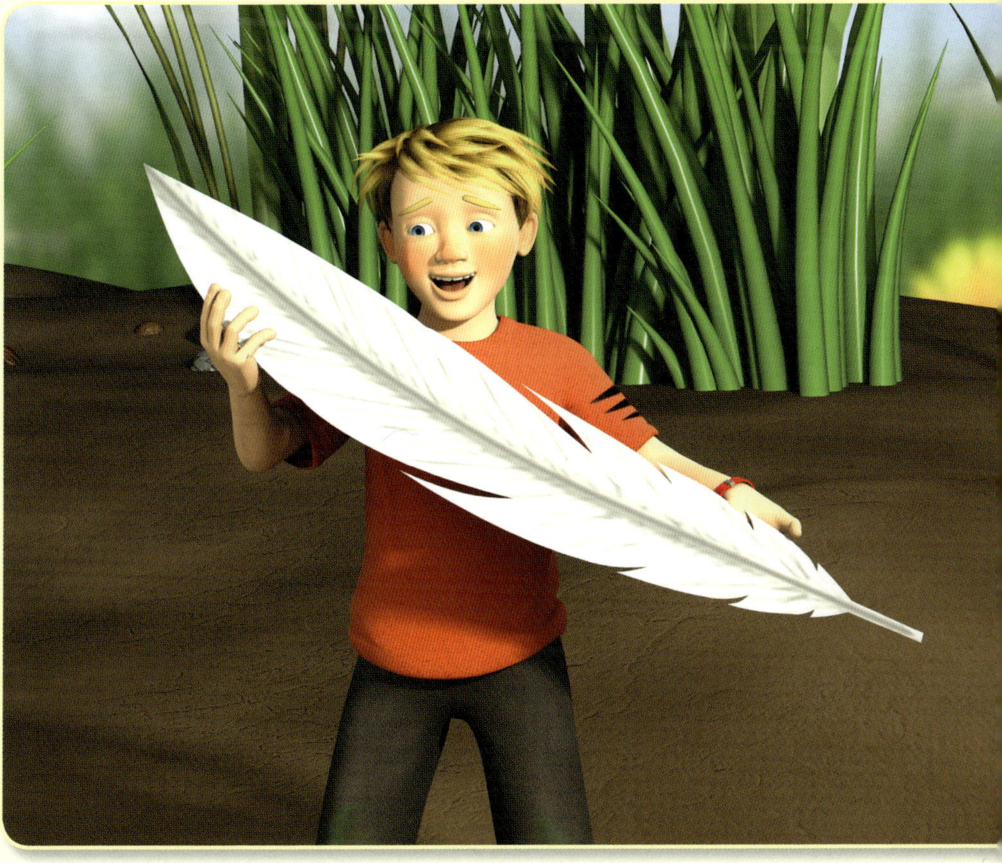

"Never fear, Tiger's here!" said Tiger. He was walking back towards Max and Ant, carrying a long, white feather. "How about this?" he said.

"Perfect!" said Max.

"That's a swan's feather!" said Ant.

"I found it at the edge of the pond," explained Tiger.

Max immediately set to work repairing the micro-copter.

In no time, Max had secured the feather in place. He strapped himself into the micro-copter again. This time, when he switched it on, his feet lifted easily off the ground.

"Good as new!" he said.

"Let's get after the cygnets," said a worried Ant. "They could be anywhere by now!"

Ant and Tiger jumped back into the micro-buggy and Tiger started the engine.

Max flew up into the air, scanning the park for signs of the cygnets. He soon spotted them. They were some way away from the pond, huddled in a group near the playground.

He signalled down to Ant, who was watching him closely from the micro-buggy. Ant then guided Tiger in the right direction.

"Oh, no!" gasped Max.

He had spotted Jack and Ben Parker. They were walking towards the playground. Their dog, Caesar, was off the lead. It was gnawing on a stick, crushing it in its strong jaws.

Max knew there was no time to lose. He just hoped they could reach the cygnets before the Parker twins spotted them.

Max dropped down. The cygnets started cheeping loudly as he circled them. They started to waddle. Max began to round them up. It was hard work as they kept going in different directions. He had to keep doubling back and doing loop-the-loops in order to keep them all together.

Just then, he heard a dog barking.

"Over there!" Jack shouted.

The twins had spotted the cygnets!

Chapter 7 – Attack!

Caesar came bounding towards the cygnets. The birds were now calling out in fright. The dog was snarling and gnashing its teeth. It was heading straight towards the smallest cygnet. The dog opened its jaws ready to bite.

All of a sudden, the micro-buggy burst out of the grass and shot between Caesar's legs. Distracted by the strange, speeding object, the dog barked, turned and set off after the micro-buggy.

"Hey," shouted Jack at his dog. "Where are you going?"

"Never mind him," said Ben. "He'll come back. We could still do with some target practice."

He picked up a large stone. He was about to throw it, when Jack saw something in the sky.

"What's that?" asked Jack.

"Uh, oh!" said Ben. Then he yelped.

The swan had heard its babies calling and had taken off in search of them. Cat was riding on the back of the swan, using the plastic hoop like a rein. She steered the swan down.

"Attack!" cried Cat, when she saw Jack and Ben.

The twins ran away as fast as they could. The swan chased after them. It hissed and screeched angrily at them and pecked at their bottoms.

Max herded the cygnets back to the pond. Minutes later, Cat and the swan came in to land. The swan glided gracefully over to its babies and soon they were all happily swimming along together.

Using all her strength, Cat pulled apart the plastic hoop so the swan would not get caught again.

Then Max picked Cat up in the micro-copter.

Ant and Tiger pulled up in the micro-buggy as Max and Cat landed.

"What happened to that horrible dog?" asked Cat.

"Oh, it was no match for my driving," said Tiger.

"Talking of which," said Max. "I think we'll call it a draw, don't you?"

The micro-friends looked down. They were all on Cat's finishing line – together.

Retell the story . . .

1

2

4

5

Find out more ...

Find out how animals get along in the wild in *Animal Conflicts*.

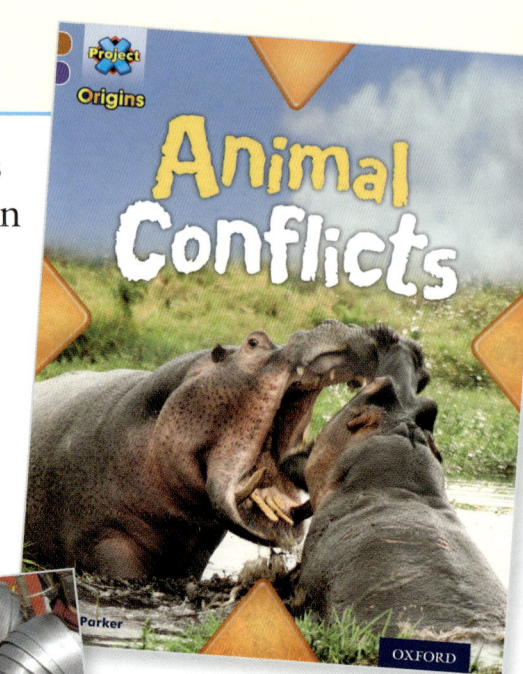

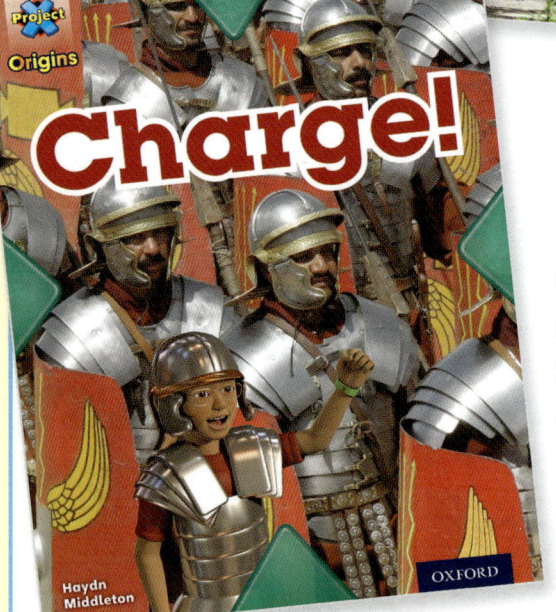

Or find out about some human conflicts through the ages in *Charge!*